Flore

You have kept photos and all sorts of mementoes
from your trips to Paris, and now you find yourself
with a unique collection, enough to awaken
your vocation to become a curator.
So as to avoid your favourite 'exhibits' getting hidden away in
an old shoe box, Elsa Editions is publishing this album
specially to give your souvenirs an ideal setting.

This interactive guide takes you back,
in text and pictures, to the atmosphere that gave
each itinerary its special charm.
You can then personalize it by including your own mementoes –
travel cards, museum tickets, restaurant menus, postcards,
bank notes etc. – in the pages designed for them.
You can include your own photos, so that the book becomes
a gentle wave of nostalgia, uniquely your own.

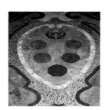

Memories

of

Florence

Florence, Capital of the Arts

Florence is probably the city that best
exemplifies the Renaissance with works
by major figures such as Botticelli,
Michelangelo, Leonardo da Vinci and
Raphael. Over the centuries, the city
has produced some remarkable
geniuses and has been associated with some of the most
prestigious names. The philosopher Machiavelli,
the poets Petrarch and Dante and the scholar Galileo
have all left their mark on the city. Florence owes
this impressive artistic and intellectual heritage
to the prosperity and ambition of its ruling princes.
Florence and the region of Tuscany were shaped
by the commercial, financial and political successes
of the powerful Medici, Strozzi and Pitti families.

The Duomo, Baptistry and Campanile

Keen to build a church that would
rival the domed cathedrals of Siena
and Pisa, the Florentines commissioned
the architect Arnolfo di Cambio
to construct their Duomo in 1296. But,
at his untimely death, only the foundations had been
completed. His successor, Giotto di Bondone, neglected
work on the cathedral in favour of the campanile. In 1337,
Francesco Talenti, who was given responsibility
for the project, revised the plans and came up with
a remarkable design.

Numerous houses were demolished to make room
for the new cathedral. But because the plans
had been extended, the Duomo seems
a little cramped in its small square.
The impressive cupola is often the only
part of the cathedral that can be
glimpsed from the narrow
neighbouring streets.

The Opera del Duomo

Behind the Santa Maria del Fiore
cathedral stands a huge building which
houses the Museo dell'Opera del Duomo.
Entirely devoted to the construction
of the cathedral, the ground floor of this
museum contains works that used to adorn the façade
of the Duomo until 1587. The mezzanine level is the home
of the Pietà, sculpted by Michelangelo when he was 24.
On the first floor, the cantorie (choir balconies), originally
situated above the Duomo's sacristy doors, are the work
of Luca della Robbia and Donatello.

Piazza della Signoria, the Heart of Florence

Piazza della Signoria has been the true hub of political and civic life in Florence since the Middle Ages. Until the 16th century, Palazzo Vecchio (the old palace) was the seat of the Florentine government and the home of much scheming and infighting… The entrance to the Palazzo Vecchio is guarded by two Florentine lions.

On the south side of Piazza della Signoria, next to Palazzo Vecchio, stands the Loggia della Signoria, also known as the Loggia dei Lanzi, in memory of the Lanzichenecchi, the German mercenaries employed as bodyguards by Cosimo I. Built to host important public ceremonies, it is now the home of various statues including Giambologna's Rape of the Sabines.

In the Shadow of Palazzo Vecchio

The history of Piazza della Signoria dates back to ancient times when it was the site of Roman baths. It was then used for popular entertainments, such as public executions. A Parlamento or mass meeting of the populace would also be summoned to the square by a peal of bells from the Palazzo Vecchio bell-tower.

This square was the arena for all the major events in the city's life. In 1498, for example, the Dominican monk Girolamo Savonarola was hanged and burned there after attempting to establish an excessively puritan, theocratic republic. The square now houses an impressive collection of statues.

Orsanmichele and Dante's District

Heading south from Piazza
del Duomo, visitors will discover
the medieval district of Florence.
This area still contains some
of the imposing towers that were used as homes
by aristocrats in the 12th and 13th centuries. The poet,
Dante Alighieri, the author of the Divine Comedy, lived
in this picturesque quarter, full of narrow streets,
passageways and stone houses, in the 13th century.

Orsanmichele is adorned by 15th-century statues
of the patron saints of the Arti or city guilds.
This church, originally built in 750 AD, owes its name

to the former oratory of San Michele
in Orto. The building on this site
was used as a grain market before
being destroyed and replaced by
the present building which finally
became a church in 1347.

Il Bargello, from Prison to Museum

The Bargello palace, with its
fine courtyard, houses
a museum containing an
excellent collection
of 15th- and 16th-century
sculptures, including pieces
by Donatello. Under the Medici
family, the palace was the home
of the police headquarters
(the barigello), from which it derives its name. From
1250, when it was built, to the 19th century, when it was
converted into a museum,
the Bargello was used exclusively
by the police and legal authorities.
In its darkest hours, this palace even
served as a prison, its cells
harbouring the most barbaric
instruments of torture.

The Uffizi Gallery, a Temple of Art

In the 16th century, Cosimo I de' Medici commissioned the architect Vasari to build the Uffizi, a building which brought together all the administrative offices. The son of Giovanni di Bicci, this art-loving despot was responsible for extending Florence's dominion by conquering the towns of Siena and Lucca. In 1581, Francis I de' Medici converted the second floor of the Uffizi into a gallery, where he displayed ancient statues, historical portraits and other masterpieces collected by his family. In 1737, the museum again grew

when Anna Maria Luisa, the last descendent of the Medici family, bequeathed the family's art treasures to the city of Florence.

Galleria degli Uffizi,
an Overview of Italian Painting

The Uffizi Gallery is Italy's most important art gallery. Its collections include major works of Italian art from the 13th to 18th centuries, presented in chronological order to illustrate the emergence and development of the Renaissance. The early stages are represented by such artists as Cimabue, Giotto and Martini. The movement becomes more firmly established with the works of Ucello, Piero della Francesca and Lippi, especially in the field of perspective. The golden age of the Renaissance is celebrated with masterpieces by Botticelli, Verrocchio and Leonardo da Vinci, and the visit is completed by the works of Bellini, Michelangelo, Raphael, Titian and Veronese.

The Mediaeval Church of Santa Croce

In 1228, a Franciscan oratory was founded in a tiny chapel dedicated to the Holy Cross. A project to entirely rebuild the church using money raised by the Inquisition was begun in 1294. However, work was continually interrupted and, when the church was dedicated in 1442, in the presence of Pope Eugene IV, it still had no façade. Even so, Santa Croce was finally able to welcome the many Florentines attracted by the austerity of the Franciscan doctrine.

In June (on one of the first Sundays and on the 24th and 28th), the vast square in front of the church, the Piazza di Santa Croce, becomes the scene of a major Florentine festival. Calcio Storico (historic football) is played by four teams dressed in the medieval livery of their district, who try to get the ball into their opponents' camp.

On public holidays and festivals,
large crowds would flock
to the Santa Croce district
to hear the Franciscans preach.
The district also attracted
the city's great artists, many
of whom are buried
in the Church of Santa Croce.
The church's many tombs
include those of such famous
historical figures as the
Florentine sculptor and painter Michelangelo,
the astronomer Galileo and the composer Rossini.
Michelangelo's body was brought back from Rome, where
he died in 1564, to be buried in Santa Croce. There are
funerary monuments to the poet Dante and the political
philosopher Machiavelli, and epitaphs commemorating

the Florentine
connections
of the artists
Raphael
and Leonardo
da Vinci.

Santissima Annunziata,
Renaissance – and Baroque – architecture

The
elegant buildings surrounding
the beautifully proportioned
Piazza della Santissima
Annunziata reflect the subtle
delicacy of Renaissance
architecture. On one side
of the square is the Ospedale
degli Innocenti, designed by
Brunelleschi. Its arcades provide
a perfect counter-balance to those of the Santissima
Annunziata, founded c. 1250 as
a Servite oratory. Opposite the church,
the Palazzo Riccardi-Manelli is one
of Florence's few brick buildings.
One side of the palace is bounded by
the slender columns of the Santissima
Annunziata whose Renaissance
interior has almost disappeared
beneath a later Baroque decor.

David in San Marco

The Galleria dell'Accademia stands on the edge of the Santissima Annunziata and San Marco districts. It is also near the University, as evidenced by the lively student presence on Piazza San Marco at all hours of the day and night. The peace and calm of the Dominican monastery of San Marco, which opens on to the square, offers a striking contrast to the noise and bustle of the surrounding streets. This beautiful building houses the major works of one of its 15th-century occupants, Fra Giovanni da Fiesole.

Fra Angelico , who became an artist late in life, decorated a number of the monastery's cells. The purity of colour and simplicity of style of his frescoes are in perfect keeping with the architecture.

San Lorenzo

San Lorenzo
is a typically
Florentine
district. Its
busy, narrow streets are pervaded by a lively and
friendly atmosphere as customers wander from shop
to shop. The magnificent Church of San Lorenzo
was created by the architect Brunelleschi
and the sculptor Donatello whose combined talents
transformed it into a 15th-century Renaissance
masterpiece. The 'Old Sacristy' is a fine example
of this successful artistic combination, with the sculpture
echoing the geometry of the architecture.

In the Princes' Chapel, the remains
of six grand dukes of Tuscany lie
in tombs of multicoloured marble.
The chapel and 'New Sacristy'
of San Lorenzo form the funerary
complex of the Cappelle Medicee
(Medici Chapel).

Michelangelo,
Architect to the Medicis

*In 1516, Michelangelo
was asked to produce a design
for the incomplete façade
of the Church of San Lorenzo.
Unfortunately, his project
was considered too costly
and the facade is still
unfinished today! However,
the Medicis commissioned
Michelangelo to create
their family mausoleum
in the 'New Sacrisity' of San Lorenzo. This was the artist's
first architectural work and he sculpted the tombs himself.*

*The dramatic impact of the tombs is remarkable
and helps to create a tragic atmosphere in which death
is viewed with resolve and determination.*

The Discreet Charm
of the Palazzo Medici-Riccardi

The austere walls of the Palazzo
Medici-Riccardi, on the Piazza
San Lorenzo, conceal an elegant
and beautifully proportioned
colonnaded courtyard.
The construction of
the 15th-century palace, built
for Cosimo de' Medici, the Elder,
involved the demolition of several
houses and the widening
of a street (the Via Cavour)
in the San Lorenzo district.

The project designed
by Brunelleschi was considered too extravagant
and Cosimo commissioned Michelozzo di Bartolomeo

to build his palazzo. Built in 1444,
the palace was sold to the Riccardi
family in 1655, when the Medicis
took up residence in the Palazzo Pitti.

Santa Maria Novella,
Where Luxury goes Hand-in-Hand with Piety

Santa Maria Novella is still
an extremely prestigious district
and the epitome of Florentine
luxury. The decoration of the Church
of Santa Maria Novella and
of the district's vast palaces
attest to the city's former wealth
and prosperity. The most powerful Florentine families
each had their own chapel in the district's many
churches. In the 15th century, Giovanni Rucellai financed
the completion of the façade – inlaid with polychrome
marble – of the Church of Santa Maria Novella, built buy
the Dominicans in the 13th and 14th centuries.

Shopping and Luxury Cafés

*During the Renaissance,
the district between the Santa
Trinità bridge and Piazza della Repubblica was
occupied by luxury drapers' shops. Today, the district's
traditional buildings house the 'trendy' boutiques
of their successors, the famous Italian designers
at the forefront of international fashion.
Even Palazzo Strozzi, the symbol of Florentine wealth,
has become involved in the luxury fashion scene
and holds the occasional fashion show.*

*In the early 20th century,
the Piazza della Repubblica's Gilli
and Giubbe Rosse cafés were
the scene of literary and artistic
debates. Today, customers are more
likely to be wearing sunglasses
than carrying books, but
the discussions are just as animated.*

Ponte Vecchio

The three arches of the Ponte Vecchio (Old Bridge) span the River Arno at its narrowest point. After the original bridge was destroyed by floods in 1333, the present Ponte Vecchio was built in 1346. It linked the city's two commercial districts and was soon occupied by shops whose occupants – tanners, fishmongers and butchers – threw their waste over the parapet, with scant regard for the state of the river. Such practices annoyed the more powerful members of Florentine society who had these professions banned from the bridge in favour

of goldsmiths and jewellers. Even so, the bridge had become so crowded by the 16th century that the Medicis had the Corridoio Vasari built above the shops. This private passageway enabled them to cross from the Palazzo Vecchio, the centre of political power, to the Palazzo Pitti in Oltrarno, without having to mingle with the crowds.

Palazzo Pitti, the Power-House of Oltrarno

In 1458, the
Florentine banker Luca Pitti
commissioned the first stage
of this magnificent building
in an ostentatious attempt to
upstage the Medicis. But,
in 1478, the Pitti family
committed a serious error when
they became involved
in an assassination attempt
against Lorenzo de' Medici. In 1540, Cosimo I de' Medici
bought the unfinished palace and had it extended.
When the Medicis took up residence,
the centre of political power was
transferred to the south bank of the
river and the Palazzo Pitti welcomed
the influential members of Florentine
society: diplomats, businessmen
and a great many courtiers.

The Delights
of the Giardino di Boboli

The long hill behind the Palazzo Pitti
was chosen by the Medicis as the site
of the Giardino di Boboli, the most
sumptuous Italian garden
of the Renaissance. It was designed by
the sculptor Niccolò de' Pericoli,
a pupil of Michelangelo, who used the
natural relief of the site to 'arrange' nature in accordance
with the design principles of the period. The Boboli
Gardens, with their many fountains and statues, draw
the visitor into the realms of romantic fantasy and it is
easy to imagine the magnificent festivities held in the
open-air amphitheatre, ensconced in a natural depression.

The Pastoral Pleasures of Florence

*The Neptune
Fountain
is one of
the many*
fountains that add their cool freshness to the Giardino
di Boboli. Near the entrance, the Bacchus Fountain,
which stands against the wall of the Palazzo Pitti,
represents the favourite dwarf of Cosimo I. Halfway
up the hillside, visitors can pause and quench their
thirst in the Kaffehaus with its picturesque 18th-century
Rococo decor. At the top of the hill, the 18th-century
Casino del Cavaliere houses the porcelain collections of
the Museo delle Porcellane.

An absolute must before leaving
Florence are the frescoes by Masaccio
in the Capella Brancacci. In 1424,
Felice Brancacci commissioned
a series of frescoes illustrating
the life of Saint Peter for what
is now the Brancacci Chapel.
The artist, Masolino, enlisted
the help of his pupil Masaccio,
who created scenes in which the force
of expression is truly remarkable.

Impressions

of

Florence

Printing Grafica Editoriale - Bologna
Dépôt légal : October 1998
(Printed in Italy)